BEFORE THE
DAWN

BEFORE THE DAWN

Poetic Reflections on Faith, Life, & Love

PETE OHLINGER

Illustrations by Daniel Scherer

To order additional copies of this book, contact:
Xlibris Corporation
1-888-795-4274
www.Xlibris.com
Orders@Xlibris.com
37718

Contents

3. Roots Digging Deeper—Part One

4. Calling Out

5. Inside and Outward

6. Roots Digging Deeper—Part Two

To my Creator, Lord, Savior, and Friend, who knew all along the path of life that would inspire me to write these pages, to my parents who raised me to know Him, and to the love of my life for whom I've been waiting all these years.

You will seek me and find me when you seek with all your heart.
Jeremiah 29:13

My Mission Statement

To become all that God has created me to be, while finding lasting fulfillment and meaning through doing His work, through a wife and family, and by using the heart, mind, and talents I've been given to make a difference in the world.

My Mission Statement

Introduction

I'd like to be able to call this book you are now holding, a labor of love. To some degree, I'll admit, it is just that. But it's perhaps more aptly described as a labor of time, and lament, and finally, love. There are moments that some pages were first penned with tears. Others were captured during a rare sense of clarity, be it practically or spiritually. And many more were written with the hope of change, of becoming someone I was not, and may still not be, and yearning for the love and companionship of a lifetime that had interminably eluded me. Some of these pages are almost shamelessly transparent, because they were written not as grandoise fodder for some future publication, but in the relative security and privacy of a personal journal. The vast majority of these pages were written by hand in a notebook that I'd kept by my bedside, often in the day's waning hours, as the need to stave the loneliness or to express something of which only words and art and music are capable.

This book began to be written over ten years ago, when I was yet a teenager. It has progressed gradually, a few seemingly unrelated pages at a time, in journal entries of mine from then until the present. It represents many of my deepest hopes and aspirations, as well as my greatest insecurities and failures. In sum, it's the melody of my soul. Even so, as I'm often surprised at the pride I feel in a few select works, I take little credit for this book at all. As these poems and prayers and lyrics and commentary have revealed myself to myself, I have come to understand both the frailty and the glory of mankind, which God the Creator has given him as His own image displays. I believe now that God must be a poet. But He is also a Master musician and artist, thinker and philosopher, inventor and entrepreneur. He is all noble qualities which we see in man's work, because His incomparable, unfathomable personality is glimpsed in understanding ourselves, His most beloved and precious creation.

I very much hope you will enjoy reading this book, not cover to cover in one sitting, unless that is what you prefer. It's also my hope that, whether young or advanced in years, a picture in your mind will be conjured up as you read a page that seems to resonate with what you're feeling at the moment, or a thought that you have not been able to express in words, or perhaps it even brings you back to something familiar that was long forgotten about yourself. I pray you will find your love for life, renewed, your mind, intrigued, and your faith, broadened. May it uplift, challenge, and identify with you, right where you are.

Introduction

I

The Longing

Life is often measured by waiting months or years for what takes place in seconds.

April Rain

When I gave my life to Him
That's when I became His kin
Not long ago I knocked again
That even more He should enter in
I felt His hand upon my life
He brought me through the weary strife
You and I under His plan
He'll bring us to the promised land

Over and over many times
Lonely streets with obscure signs
And if what I've found in you
Is in His will, then it is true
'Cause if I know of you or not
The one for me is worth the cost
Of waiting on His every word
Because I know hope is not lost
With skillful hands He uses hurt
And joy to bring His plan to earth

I will send down showers in season; there will be showers of blessing.
Ezekiel 34:26

Drink Me In

You know what I want
It's what I'll always be
But aside from that
Is personality

Eyes wide with sincere interest
At the petty things I say
Head tilted in compassion
As I talk of a hard day

A note left on the table
Saying I love you
An expectant outstretched hand
And arms of gratitude

Receptive to my gifts
And holding nothing back
Feeling lucky as I do
For having time with you to chat

Simplicity of honesty
At letting me inside
To discern your deepest fears
Sharing all, nothing to hide

Just knowing that your heart
Has room for me to fit
Even with all my faults
You've decided to commit

I don't know who or when
Or if I've met you yet
But pray for me as I for you
So that you'll not forget

I sit and wait
For as long as I need
To make certain I've found you
To know that what we have is true

Drink me in
As I pour myself out
Let me try to whisper
With a shout

Immense

If you tried to contain my love in the ocean
Or put it in the sky
There'd be no room for fish to swim
Or for the birds to fly
My love for you is so very vast
It looks down on every mountain
If you buried it deep within the ground
It would burst into a fountain

If my love for you could be contained
It could only be in space
But soon, inevitably it would
Push the stars from out their place
As grand as my love must sound to you
It's sadly not returned
Even though when I should think of you
My heart is stirred and churned

If there were a name to call my love
There's but one name to be found
But what words when spoken could name my love
Without you, words make no sound

Moments Like in Movies

Many a night, grown weary
At the thoughts, the wishing I feel
When I think of what it will be like
To have you next to me

I know that not a day goes by
That some glimmer of you shines
Within a corner of my mind
As I see others, lovers entwined

I'm not certain which has been harder
Disappointment or the waiting
I've done my share of both
And I've seen the toll it's taking

Sometimes I've often buried
The longing deep inside
But in moments like in movies
It comes out in tears I've cried

There's no telling just what I'll do
Just how grateful to my Lord
I will feel when you are with me
Finally, loneliness no more

With great anticipation
I pray you're drawing near
God's hand of great provision
Has made your vision clear

Scarcely able in containing grandeur
So great as what we'll share
What blessings God will pour out
In a love beyond compare

Hollywood

A screen of colors, the forms and shapes
The portrayal of the perfect one
It tells the how, it tells the way
To get the one, and make her stay
It shows the weak and sensitive
The one who wins, who gets to live
But hardly is it real enough
For me even to believe that stuff
The flashy, cool, and jocular
Always the center of popular
It's hard to meet, it's hard to find
The Hollywood romantic kind

Within

There's no way to understand
How could you be let go?
When I think of how amazing you are
I can't help but let it show

You're the reason I've held on
To the hope inside my heart
You're the gift I prayed to be given
And I can't wait for it to start

If this is all I'm praying for
It to be meant to be
There's nothing I won't do for you
You can always count on me

When I think about from where we came
To where we seem to be
No one else has understood
Me like you have with me

You're the fire that never died
Even when the light was dim
You're the lover at my side
That lights me up within

Surrender

The bitter sting of tears I've cried
A sign the hope within me died
I know I'm still a friend
I know it's not the end

But it's hard for me to separate
The memories from the mistakes
And where did I go wrong
Could I have seen this come

There's solace in the lonely fact
That you're not gone except for that
Which I must now let you go
In my heart down deep below

I wish there were some other way
To cling to hope without betray
But I've seen hope's wound so deep
For the second time, it seems

Now what's hard is how I live
Differently than before, than this
Revelation I didn't want
But used it still, God did, to haunt
My every step, my every move
What I've gained from you I can never lose

And still I know there's no way I
Could not fall in love, nor let you inside
You've changed me now, forevermore
I hope I've held, though still not sure
God's hand may now have closed the door
I surrender, His will, I do implore

Not So Young

I know when I was young, as I learned about myself
A side of me that still remains
Was growing but not in health
Little did I know that every romantic fantasy
Of holding hands and kissing lips
And reading notes endlessly
Would start the building of an altar, an idol in my heart
A place that put God a distant second
And true blessings chained to the start

I was bewildered how could I feel
A closeness like some sweet girl's appeal
I thought that intimacy only resides
In love songs, long walks, and starry eyes
But now it's been revealed to me
That my lonely days were meant for me to see
That God can be more than just a friend
Or a heavenly helper with a perpetual grin
He's showing me intimacy
That I thought would be only between a wife and me
Was meant for us to share
And to be more valued than any other care

So Father, I offer up this prayer
Hasten the call upon my heart
To break idolatrous chains, to finally start
To love You first and always most
That when the time comes to be not alone
I'll have all the best it could become
And expressed within that marriage with her
Gratitude to You, my first love, endures

Haikus and Tankas

A rose and softer
Growing, changing, beautiful
Rises to the sun

Like garden tended
A breath of life beginning
And we flourish so

Spinning round and so
Encapsulated and not
Obscure, let life's needs
In, and in a moment's time
We have found eternity

Falling faster through
New space and new memories
Making, little fear
Of what's beyond we cling and
Anticipate the unknown

The Writers

The Writers chit chat amongst themselves
Ideas flicker and bounce like a flame
But most things have stayed the same
A subtle glance at a passerby
Nevertheless a glint in their eye
As they watch inside the churning minds
Involuntary flinch as the door opens
Steady as a footstep, they keep their cool
Trying not to break the unwritten rule
But it's too late, they have noticed her face
And captivation unnerves their conversation
In a panic they attempt the discussion
It falters silent as their minds unhitch
She's already seen their watchful eye
Quiet whispers fill the room
Like an aroma of the future soon
Dare they ask a question, dare they speak a word
Tensions fall heavy as their thoughts converge
Until their number drops to two
As the others stare in blatant view
He approaches but utters not a sound
Her head flips left, the chair spins round
Their hands reach in pockets and fumble about
Searching for the writ and spout
They exchange the parchment, then one heads out

Second Wind

In the dizzying effect of light and sound
Two strangers, two sets of eyes set down
A fleeting glance, a lost romance
Someone passing by
With a glint in their eye
You may get a smile, you may get a dance
The number on the card, by chance
But in the midst of nightly wonder
Behind the beat and blaze asunder
It seems so hard to find a plane
Where it won't fall as random drops of rain
And sitting, resting, by yourself
You stop to breathe back to your health
And give a slow eye to the crowd
That seems so cold, like November clouds
And there you see groups formed in pairs
Your compliment not in nearby chairs
But ever-pressing, back on the floor
You mount your courage
And try once more

Why I Love You Like I Do

This love I feel for you
Unshaken, strong, and true
I can't understand why it won't let go
It hopes and cries and begs
It yearns in desperate prayers
Only to see you through

'Cause I know the Savior's love
Is reaching out to you
It's been placed in my heart
That's why I love you like I do

Many times I've thought, that I can't explain
Just why it is I can't give up
You're like a jewel to me, priceless in your beauty
I won't leave until the Lord is done
No, I can't quite explain
Why I am willing to feel the pain
To keep putting myself on the line
Maybe because, I pray in time
Soon is your salvation day

What We Could Be

The light upon your hair it blinds my eyes
I burn inside and give my heart to you
And so it seems that all the love is mine
We are together but a distance grew

It know it happened when we were apart
I'm not sure if you feel the same for me
You forced the love in my transparent heart
Just think, if you gave more, what we could be

I feel I'm only holding on to you
You hold on loosely and you take my all
Please open up your heart to me it's true
Why be afraid just tear down all your walls

I could not hurt or ever leave your side
How much you mean to me I cannot hide

Fade

Tears still fall at the refrain
Memories that have been replayed
I breathe in deep and clutch my chest
Lonely when my heart finds rest

I wonder if I could compare
One love to another or even measure
What scale could tell the height of pleasure
What line would note what we have shared

It's hard for me to venture forth
When you've shown me what life is worth
The loneliness has crept back in
At times I hate the hole I'm in

I was a better person when
You filled the role of romantic friend
It seems to me my colors fade
When no one sees each hue and shade

The Lord is close to the brokenhearted and saves those who are crushed in spirit.
Psalm 34:18

Becoming

Every tear and laugh I hold
They wait for arms that fold into yours
Every moment I become
Is all to give you every one
Of my faults, my flaws, my weaknesses
You inspire my strength with acceptance
You're a place I go to find relief
You're the help I seek when there's no peace
These days, all I'm doing is saving up
I'm becoming all you're going to love
The hardest thing is not sharing yet
Those things I hope I won't forget
But pleasant is the thought of hope
That one day I'll not have to cope
Any longer for the solitude
Is done, and life begins with you

*And hope does not disappoint us, because God has poured out his
love into our hearts by the Holy Spirit, which he has given us.*
Romans 5:5

When You're Lost

When you're lost, the sun doesn't sparkle
And moonbeams hold no gratitude for a nightly stroll
When you're lost, time passes too quickly
And too slowly all at once
When you're lost, no comfort is felt
And no joy is found

It's as if you scream but make no sound
It's the thought of air before you drown
It grips your focus and snuffs the light
It sends you falling, sprawling, hoping, grasping
For the end of every sleepless night

I can't be normal, I can't move on
My heart is broken, placed upon
The altar where I fuel the fire
The pains with each care desired
And fueled by every wall let down
As if to wear a thorned crown
By searching for a thing so grand
That breaks your back and burns your hand

I'd forgotten what it was like to live
Wishing for distraction's sieve
To leak the ill, discomforted
To give me rest inside my head

I care too much, I love too deep
To let the gift slip from her reach
And all that holds my head above
Is trusting in a God of love

When I'm lost and cannot find my way
When I'm broken, bruised, and hurt each day
When I wish to give this yoke away
Comfort is found each time I pray

Advent

There was a time
When self pity was my drug
I could live only inside myself
Hurt made me blind
And senses came alive
I would think of nothing else

Time has shown me level ground
A season of non-event
But I'm ready now to begin
Bring me to passion's advent

If You'll give me the chance
I will place You high above
I will make circumstance
Serve You with purest love

I'm ready now to open up
Awaken my heart's sleep
Let new love bring forth Your plan
Lead me unto the deep

I have the chance to spring forth from
This safe unfeeling place
Let me find love for real this time
Until I see Your face

Show me how to leave behind
My false securities
Empty my will of selfish gain
Let me first find favor with Thee

Grant my wish, my heart's desire
Your words and song through me
Find in me a burning fire
That longs for purity

Bestow on me opportunity
To serve You with my gift
Let me know for sure I've found the one
That I'll spend my life with

Delight yourself in the Lord, and he will give you the desires of your heart.
Psalm 37:4

Just in Time

I closed my eyes just long enough to dream
I saw your face next to mine
I couldn't tell you what I hope it means
But I'm sure I'll know, just in time

If there's more than I can imagine
Waiting for us in His hands
If all I've known for certain
Brought us together in His plan
If all those boyhood longings
Were used to shape this man
Then I'm sure we'll both know, just in time

If I could open up a page to give a better look
Then you'd see one jewel in thousands
In your gift, my heart-song's book
There could be no way a lifetime
For to read each page of me
Would be enough to show all
Of what I'm saving up for thee

When it's our time—we'll know
When the wait is all gone—He'll show
Us why it took the path it did
For me to find you just in time

Writing Our Love Story

I wonder if the time has come
Are all the waiting years now gone
Is this the moment I was made
For more than my sin's serenade
I listen for the voice of truth
That carries me to man from youth
I've strayed when flesh its weakness fails
Yet crawl I do back unto You, nailed

There is the dream that still remains
A longing inside full of pain
I find myself still clinging to
The vision of a dream come true

And so I wonder if the time has come
If she is now revealed to me
Have all the days from here and gone
Been written in God's love story

Are You writing as my pen displays
The visage of a patient sage
Are You writing now our love story
Your pen unfolds its work in glory

The Master's Pen

Everything I've always wanted
The things I've wanted most
It hasn't been just about me
It means more than just my vote

So say I find myself one day
No longer dreaming more
It doesn't mean You've kept Your bargain
For some widow's darkened door

No, the things that drive the very words
I pray to You each day
Are hardly ends in of themselves
But insist for to proclaim

That every detail, large and small
Every hope and every trial
Every joy that speaks of Your Name on high
And bids my soul to smile

My everything, my all in all
The story that's unfolding
Was penned so masterfully to tell
The glory You've been holding

II

The Heart Overflowing

It's the hope that hurts, because it reminds of what you do not yet have . . . .

Now I Know

I can't reason this at all
Nor figure out how I've recovered from the fall
Inside a minute my world came crashing down
Then the next He wiped my tears
And took away my frown

Now I know
Why did I have to grieve
Now I know
To trust His sovereignty

Before I couldn't see the forest for the trees
Like an eclipse aligns itself
So my heart became down on my knees
And suddenly the veil of doubt has lost its fear
Optimistically I know
My future He holds dear

Now I know
The pain turned to release
Now I know
What it's like to be set free

Change and Wait

Someone's broken down my escape
Look for windows and doors to break
Don't understand why I should die
It's been done before, not a lie

But it's not too long to change and wait
I could leave myself and feel betrayed
Only heaven's arms can help me see
The change is inside, it's inside of me

So much is gone, but there's more to behold
Your second wind will come, I've been told
His evil whispers can break you down
Unless you're standing on solid ground

But it's not too long to change and wait
I could leave myself and feel betrayed
Only heaven's arms can help me see
The change is inside, it's inside of me

Man looks at the outward appearance, but the Lord looks at the heart.
1 Samuel 16:7

Inner Seal

Where does it end when you feel you've lost yourself
Where to begin when the toll takes more than wealth
I want to be the one I used to be
I want to send the love to you from me
Don't want to lose sight of what I know I am
Throw out the old, distorted habits of mine

I don't want to lose it all
Being real it makes you strong
Honesty the policy
True to oneself and to one's God

Sometimes it takes a heartfelt story or two
To introspect your life and what you must do
I want to hold on to the treasure in me
I want to give of myself so freely

Pieces

Here I am again, I've let you down, my friend
I took up my cross for awhile
But I've lost my vision

I had something good with You
And I've severed the tie so true
But I can't believe that this is the end
I need You to help me back up again

'Cause I'm picking up the pieces
If only to find myself where I can meet You
Draw me deeper, my Redeemer
Till all I can see is your face and your glory 'round me

Father, I don't know what's to come of me
The life that you call me to lead seems so far from reach
But I'm digging, digging deeper
And I'm praying, praying for your touch

'Cause I'm picking up the pieces
If only to find myself where I can meet You
Draw me deeper, my Redeemer
Till all I can see is your face and your glory 'round me

You make me beautiful
You fill my life to full
I know I can trust You
'Cause no one loves me like You do

'Cause I'm picking up the pieces
If only to find myself where I can meet You
Draw me deeper, my Redeemer
Till all I can see is Your face and Your glory 'round me

Dreaming Awake

Somehow you always bring me to my knees
There's no way I can turn my heart away
I've let you go, and yet you still return to me
Is there a plan to make you stay

But I'm dreaming awake
If I let you go again
I'm dreaming awake
If there's another way

Every time you call, there's a smile inside
I try to show you all I am is real
Someday I wish you'd see me as I am
No place I'd rather be than at your side

But I'm dreaming awake
If I let you go again
I'm dreaming awake
If there's another way

You are inside of me, I'll never let you go
There's no hiding me, my transparency
One day the blind will see, the Lord will make a way
One day your life will change, as surely as I pray

The Immeasurable

It's hard to think, to calculate
Just how much we have lost
Potential of the grandest scale
Fulfillment never known
It's just too sad and hard to bear
To watch one throw away their life
But most don't know, their eyes are shut
What matters is disgraced

I don't want to sacrifice
One day, or waste one breath of mine
That contains the immeasurable
Gifts from the Divine

I'm learning now how not to judge
It's true you reflect me
What imaginary line I've yet to cross
Is lack of opportunity
And I'm starting now, just starting
To really comprehend, all the truth
I only thought I knew
It's here my life begins

I don't want to sacrifice
One day, or waste one breath of mine
That contains the immeasurable
Gifts from the Divine

Revelation

I had a revelation
The reason that You made creation
The deepest longing inside me
Is the reason You made me

You long to love and be loved
You love to have our time, our hearts
You made us so You could enjoy us
And You cry too, when we depart

I had a revelation
The reason that You made creation
The deepest longing inside me
Is the reason You made me

I know the reason now You made me
Deep unto deep, to value those around me
To want to share my life faithfully
This in common, we share creatively

I had a revelation
The reason that You made creation
The deepest longing inside me
Is the reason You made me

You desire to love and be loved
It's the same desire You gave me from above
'Cause the greatest thing I want in this life
To have a home, family, and wife

I had a revelation
The reason that You made creation
The deepest longing inside me
Is the reason You made me

Wandering One

I was losing my way, feeling like I was a child again
When You, Lord, meant much less to me, less to me, than now
I cannot go back, I've got to let truth shine its way through
You call me to be set apart, God let me depart from this . . .

From falling away, falling into old ways
Falling away into . . .

My struggle within, when I chose to ignore
The emptiness I felt from my own sin
When I chose to disobey, and heard You pleading with me
You gave me the strength, but I threw it away
And the next voice I heard was them laughing at me, well, no more

I was falling away, Lord help me this day
Jesus I pray, strengthen this wandering one
This wandering one

You call me to read, to soak in the deep
Your wisdom is within my reach
So God give me the stand, let fear lose its hand
And bless me in ways I can't conceive, and don't deserve

They're falling away, one by one
While I hold the cure in my heart
I'm falling away somehow
Show me where I must start

Let me long for You, only for You
'Cause they're falling away

Sanctify

I have felt the rush of sin's desire
I have spit upon what I believe
I have pushed away when I should cleave
My blackened heart yet does conspire

I have lifted up my arms in worship
I have spoken out for Your cause
I have carried to the proud Your laws
But all my deeds are simply worthless

Say unto me
I have not once believed
Oh, say unto me
I'm in need of Your reprieve

I will offer the only gift I can
I will reach out to Your outstretched hand
I am ready to accept Your plan
Sanctify—I am only man

Say unto me
Use my life as You please
Oh, sanctify
Don't let me stand and watch them die
Don't let me, don't let me stand and watch them die
Oh, sanctify; put a tear within my eye

Precious Friend

My God, look what I've done to You
Laid bare, what a sight to view
Purity takes the blame
Pain unreal, Your Father looks away

I could never understand
How they could take this man

Justice done unto the undeserved
Spilled blood, life reserved
Don't let me sin again
Look what I've done to You, my Precious Friend

I could never understand
With a frail human mind
What love with a plan
Could save all humankind

My God, look what I've done to You
Laid bare, what a sight to view
Purity takes the blame
Pain unreal, Your Father looks away

I could never understand
With a frail human mind
What love with a plan
Can save all humankind

Don't want to wait to be near
Please just take me from here
My Precious Friend
My Precious Friend

Stuck or Set

This is what happens when I don't cling to You
Step out of bounds, lose my place, feel the glue
Gotta maintain, can't control what I do
Let me sustain, give me boldness and truth

Set apart for Him
Not like the rest within
Can't go back, old ways let me down
Turn away, without air, and I drown

The narrow road is filled with vines
The travelers few with many left behind
Stuck in a life, perpetual sin
He'll break the chains if you'll just be

Set apart for Him
Not like the rest within
Can't go back, old ways let me down
Broken dreams and a broken crown

Will you be stuck or set
Strange enough you seem to forget
He'll show you how to let habits die
Be your friend to no end, be your guide

Water to Wine

Holding my breath till I am blue
Waiting in line for one like you
Still in a room without a view
Hoping to find that this is true

Praying each day will keep the time
Holding the beat, the song, the rhyme
Wishing your heart will turn to flesh
From Him you'll find only the best

Pouring myself out like a glass
Looking into a sorrowed past
Haven't a clue if it'll last
Giving myself a second chance

I wish that you will be with me
Each night I'm down on bended knee
Praying to God that you'll receive
His love and life eternally

You drag me down into the fire
Shaping my life's one true desire
Bring me closer to Your feet
Holding a light to those I meet

Seven years or seven days
Time is wasted without grace
Suddenly, the heart and mind
Stone to flesh, water to wine

Save You

When your days have got you down
When you can't find a moment's peace
Just remember, you never have to go it alone
You can find all the rest that you need

Let me be your crying shoulder
Let me be your waiting arms
I just can't let you by, when you're hurting inside
I would give all I have in this life . . . to save you

Heaven knows what the future may hold
And just why we've become what we are
But if I had my way, for just how much you would stay
I pray that you'd never be very far

I want to rescue you, save and protect you
Make every dream come true

Let me be your crying shoulder
Let me be your waiting arms
I just can't let you by, when you're hurting inside
I would give all I have in this life . . . to save you

Clarity

In this world it's hard not to become
A slave to all things that fill our days
I try so hard to remember what it's like
To be so full of life, to gaze with pure delight

I've been reminded of peace
Contentment close to me
Take the time it takes to see
With perfect clarity

Find a friend who you are sure to keep
Pray for love that you have never known so deep
Know who you are then build up a dream
Rest in the watchful eye that keeps you as you sleep

I've been reminded of peace
Contentment close to me
Take the time it takes to see
With perfect clarity

The fear of the Lord leads to life: then one rests content, untouched by trouble.
Proverbs 19:23

Been Dreaming

I've been thinking, how does romance fit in
When all that God's planned has His fingerprints
Just trying to make sense, to know what to do next
I want to lay it all down, to find the place of rest

So many nights I've been dreaming of you
So many prayers spent thinking of you
There must be a way that this heart can keep going
To find you in God's perfect time
To find you

Thought of calling you at midnight
Just to say that you've been on my mind
So scared to let myself drift once again
And I'm not sure, no, not sure if I can

My heart isn't made for today
It's made for always with you
And He's got a way, when it's all okay
Of showing Himself to be true

So many nights I've been dreaming of you
So many prayers spent thinking of you
There must be a way that this heart can keep going
To find you in God's perfect time
To find you

Surely, as I have planned, so it will be, and as I have purposed, so it will stand.
Isaiah 14:24

Best That's Ever Been

I've never had nobody like you
But I know this ain't the time
Darlin' I can't help but love you
Now is my lovin' such a crime

Now don't you know
I'd wait for you, the end of time

Surely there has never been
A better girl for me
As sure as I can tell, my darlin'
Ain't no way there'll ever be

Now don't you know
You're the best that's ever been

Now I'm not here just pickin' flowers
There's no roses in my eyes
When I tell you I can't help but love you
It's the truth, it's no disguise

Now can't you see
Baby, you belong with me

Surely now just as I'm breathin'
There's been no better friend
There is no one that I would rather
Love my whole life to the end

Now can't you see
You're the best that's ever been
Now don't you see
I'm in love with my best friend

A Love Song

Lord, You've molded me from all You've given me
And given me aspiring character
You have set me on the path of wisdom, and drawn my heart to You

And I feel at home when You surround me
I feel at peace when You draw me in
Jesus, my life, let it be a love song
Let all I am sing praise to You

Oh God, You are teaching me what it means to truly worship
Oh Lord, You're changing this heart of mine
In You I find sanctuary
Your every word like sweetest wine

And I feel at home when You surround me
I feel at peace when You draw me in
Jesus, my life, let it be a love song
Let all I am sing praise to You

In those times when I've forgotten
When I have wandered willingly
Your tender heart radiates mercy
And I claim the blood that covers me
I claim the blood that sets me free

And I feel at home when You surround me
I feel at peace when You draw me in
Jesus, my life, let it be a love song
Let all I am sing praise to You

I will sing to the Lord all my life; I will sing praise to my God as long as I live.
Psalm 104:33

I Will Fall

For years it seems, I've been stretched out in the desert
The water, scarce, it seems, a mirage of chasing dreams
The sun beats down, my hope deferred
My heart grows sick within my fragile world
But hope's not gone
It won't be long
I'll sing a new song

I believe a time will come
Blessings flowing like a flood
I cannot stand, I will fall
To my knees in awe of what You've done

These lessons learned, how they take place
Is there no other way to live a life of faith
The growing pains of stubborn man
You let me fall to show Your master plan
No, hope's not gone
It won't be long
I'll sing a new song

I believe a time will come
Blessings flowing like a flood
I cannot stand, I will fall
To my knees in awe of what You've done

To my knees in praise
To my knees in awe
At the glory You've saved up for me
The glory as I wait on Thee
To my knees will I fall
When I see it all, when you reveal it all
I will fall

Hope deferred makes the heart sick, but a longing fulfilled is a tree of life.
Proverbs 13:12

III

Roots Digging Deeper
Part One

You are never more than a day past how you have lived yesterday.

Lasting change begins with building on what you do today.

A Word Defined

I am but a word, and You are the dictionary that contains me.

In You I have meaning; in You I find my place.

In You I find where I fall in the order of things.

You are what defines me.

Because You are, then I am here.

You list my purpose, and by the definition You give of me, I find usefulness, reason, and destiny.

I am but a word, uttered into existence by Your will.

You call me by name, and my name finds its meaning in You.

For in him we live and move and have our being.
Acts 17:28

Sever the Past

When I was young, I hid my face
From mountainous tasks that stood in my way
I slept, I ran, watching and wasting
The hours and days were all bland tasting
There were fleeting moments of recourse
But hardly enough effort was made, of course

I'm still there, on the chairman's board
Head of the fleece of time and more
But without the books, classrooms, and pens
Absent of teachers or schoolmates as friends
I'm constantly in the recovery room
With all the dreams, yet no will to move
My mind feels as though it's still in pieces
I move in vain toward a faint horizon
Only to find mirage in place of oasis
Sand to quench my thirst, rocks as my libation
I'm still in the same situation
I tell myself, "You've done this or that"
Or, "Look at the place you're at"
But have I made any progress at all
With time on the clock, just holding the ball

I've abandoned my God, I've gone my own way
I've given myself up in a selfish display
I'm a fitting example of one called backslidden
I'm a waste of potential, talent so given
My soul stirs at the slightest sound
Familiar neighbors to my frown
Are dreary eyes and a burdened crown
My Lord, what have I done to You
I'm as fickle as a child of two
You've set me free, but I choose to stay
Locked in my mediocre chains
I live in shame, and lack real faith
I'm not worthy to even bear Your name
Help me, please, supernaturally
Bring my pride down to its knees
Sever the past, and give me peace

So Much

Something more than to wade
In a sea of mediocrity
I want to soar high above
The tallest tree

Take hold of God's hand
And let Him lift me
Tired of the empty hole
That used to be

Give me something I can't stand
To live without—Your endless perfect plan
Of love will break the scales

Let me feel the wind blow on new skin
Let me take upon myself
As long as it's better than this

Don't let me waste any more time
Or settle for the daily grind
There so much more, I know
I want something more

Restoration

I don't know why
But it feels like I'm on the outside looking in
Trying to decide if I belong
Finding that the veil I wear is thin

I see my mistakes
When I realize the more that time has passed
I seem to blend in with this world
Knowing that the light I hold is black

I want gifts beyond imagination
But severed is the fascination
Of knowing I'm treasured creation
Bring it back to me
Bring me to my knees

Have I doubted grace
Have I let my guilt destroy what I can be
I have wasted much
But there is still much that I can be

I want a Holy transformation
Cover me with a strange fixation
Build me up, prepare me for battle, send me out
Pour Your love, give me identity without a doubt

My Glory Due

I take this charge, within my hand
Being fully Yours, yet fully man
Past failures gone, present struggles wane
If I each day my heart reclaim
I am new within, I am born again
I am not the sinner ruled by sin
I am a child of God, a brethren saint
Called to bear my Father's Name
My heart is good, it's been transformed
It finds freedom when sin ignored

For so long now, I have lost heart
I've believed the lies of sin within
I've lived much less than my true self
And I've found such life devoid of health
Its course is shame, its reward hollow
An emptiness that is hard to swallow

But truth's winds blow, to push back the fog
Revealing the gaze of prison gates unlocked
So I venture forth, as one set free
No need to remain where I used to be
Now it's time to find what life awaits
As I clamber to a stream to bathe
Dirt washes off, and my body made clean
The water calms and my reflection seen
I see the man I've always been
No longer covered from the dirt of sin
My soul reclaimed, my heart made new
To live to see my glory due

*Therefore if anyone is in Christ, he is a new creation;
the old has gone, the new has come!*
2 Corinthians 5:17

The Desperate Voice

What more can I say to You, Lord
When my heart grows tired as the days go by
Desperation creeps upon me
And steals my peace away
I have seen a change in me
Though gradual it has been
But I have grown in a great many ways
Inside You're making me clean

Now half a year's gone by
I hardly notice one more day
Inside the desperate voice sounds faint
And I wonder, will my hope fade
I don't want to give up just yet
When I'm so near to purity
I want the best God has to offer
To see His grace in you and me

Path to Conviction

How could I let the light be covered
By the darkness of this world
How could I have been so blind to compromise Your ways

And how did I not see
My seeds sown in destruction
I have stained the reputation of the One I love the most

My God, my precious Jesus
Forgive this sinner's heart
Had I listened to Your words of wisdom
Lives might not have fallen apart

I see so clearly now, as one of Your true servants spoke
That I cannot in any way
Be unequally yoked
For to walk in the ways of righteousness
And avoid snares of the past
I will turn my eyes above
And make straight this narrow path

What Good?

What good is being educated, if you lack wisdom?

And what good are theorems and proofs, if you do not have understanding?

What good are policies and procedures, if you lack discernment?

What good is punctuality and productivity, if you haven't the sense to
prepare your own soul for when it will be required of you?

What good is adherence to rules and regulations, if you have not first
bowed down before the one True King?

And what good is wealth or possessions, if your own heart is bankrupt?

Making New

Mediocrity my destiny
If I seek not Your will for me
My place is second best
If I choose to fail to this test

Stolen from my soul possession
Like a gift never given
Write me off and on I go
Blessing into oblivion

How could I sacrifice what's within me
Something greater than I has gotten to me
I serve the God above before any man below
I'm much different now, you know

I pray for evidence of softened hearts
I seek the path that few have trod
I pray to finally live for You
This process burns the skin while making new

Reckless Love

There is a love that will never abandon
The lost one whose heart is afraid
And there is a reason for seasons of waiting
While you're begging to God to come save

I'm am learning how
You love so recklessly
I can see You now
Your heart laid bare on the tree

This is the time where I'm being tested
To place all my cares upon Him
When I can't see why it's all taking so long
Your work keeps on moving within

Vulnerable, aching, longing inside
To see the sinner set free
Powerful, wonderful, all in good time
The prayers of the righteous will be
Sorrowful, painfully, frustration sets in
When I think just when will she see
Miracles, mysteries, His heart divine
One day the heart will be redeemed

Hope for the Lost

More than conquerers
We are through You
Hope for the lost
Love at all cost
Never ashamed
Souls are at stake

So take the sickle, pick the fruit
The harvest ready, the workers few
They shall know what they've done to You
Remind us Lord, what we've done to You

So gather us up, send us out
And it's for Your name we shout
They will know why it is
That they've got need of forgiveness

They need to know Your love
They need to see Your face
We must know we've done You wrong
In our weakness, make us strong

Today, if you hear His voice, do not harden your hearts . . . .
Hebrews 3:7-8

Waiting in Heaven

When she was young, the house was filled
With abuse of nearly every kind
A mother who could not control her anger
When she had too much wine
A father hardly known
One who was barely there
This young child, this precious girl
Had scars on her heart bare

She needed to feel the love and warmth
From anyone she could find
And so she married oh so young
During so tender a time
But soon her soul had seen enough
Of abuse from this man too
His words had cut her down too much
She knew to leave him soon
Her longing heart and fragile state
Led her from one to another
During which time, if it weren't enough
She lost her own dear mother

When we first met I tried to help
Compassion filled my heart
I tried to lead her to the Lord
I prayed she'd find a fresh start
Too soon she left, my pain was deep
The hurt would linger on
I tried not to let the bitterness
Make me weak instead of strong
So I reached out to make it clear
That a friend I'd always remain
But she needed to let her Father in heaven
Wipe away all the pain

The Father cries out each day for this child
He wants to wrap His arms around her
And calm the ways gone wild
If she could only see how much
The Father loves her so
This child she will bear in time
Is a piece of heaven's gold
This circumstance which He allowed is yet opportunity
For her to stop running away from
The only Father she'll ever need

He died for her, if that's not enough
He begs to hear her say
"Father, can you love me after how I've lived today?"
His answer, quick, and with great love
"I've never stopped loving you, my child."
Then He asks the question
"Will you love me back this time?"

This is where the story awaits conclusion
It's her decision now
And so the Father waits in heaven
Until her hand reaches out

He Cries Silently

Clouded, hardened, depraved, confused
Or ironically found in a pew
Subtlety of a gentle knock
At the door to your heart is not heard

He stands in quiet, patiently
Awaiting the return of thee
Wincing at the path we choose
Did you know that He cries silently

Wrought and formed, as in a mold
I share the tragic line He towed
But never could I know the pain
He feels for each life lived in vain

He wants you to know, as I do too
What life is like turned 'round by truth
I pray, someday, your eyes will see
Each day, for you, He cries silently

But God demonstrated his own love for us in this:
While we were still sinners, Christ died for us.
Romans 5:8

Need

Sweet peace is my release
Strange that I have taken You for granted
Captured soul should be my goal
Why so much of this life I've wasted

Caught in the whirlwind of this world
The apple of my eye has bought my burden
You should have been my focus
For what I fight hid by this curtain

The masses fall to their death
And I haven't helped but one
The mercy moves at Your breath
I've got to try to make them listen

Fire, pain, and torture
Await those who heed not this warning
Taken in the rapture
Those hearts Your name are bearing

What love is this that sent His son to die
To break our selfish pride and let Him occupy
The space within to cover sin
With perfect sacrifice

All you've done to live in purity
Is as the swine who wallows deep
Please listen as the Father speaks through me
He wants to give you life eternally

Given Up

My mind is numb and I'm sick of this routine
Make my brain play dumb, keep my outside clean

Blocked out from a freedom that should be mine
I feel the weight crash down on me
Hear the crack of my spine

It is not my burden to take, I have in You my own escape
Giving up is not giving in, when it's a prayer given up to You

Strange how it seems I'm so fragile inside
One blow I'm fine, two I'll run and hide

Sweet release as Your plans unfold
Heaven's gate, mercies untold

Reason and Rhyme

While it's easier to crawl in a hole
Than to strive for purpose and a goal
I cannot abandon my post
Nor give up on what I value most

I can only live each minute through
The past is done, the future, new
I introspect in retrospect
And try to keep my heart in check

Deceitful, wandering, and blind
I set upon the path to find
A better way than now to live
Not to forget what care I give

In finding myself in shallow pools
Of thought, the deep becomes so cruel
It lets you not out of its hold
Its prison cell, character's mold

And never can we grow mature
By passing things off, knowing for sure
Instead the tread of soul searched long
Footsteps that twist and turn in song

Disheartened can one who has not the love
Of Christ's redeeming power above
Jump off the train of duty's call
Set foot against the stone and fall

To never have been burdened by
The load of moods that will not die
Unless they're quenched by thought and time
Would give life no reason or rhyme

The Musician

He's different than the average man
His mind is wired so
Creatively articulating
Thoughts that most don't know

He's stubborn and prideful
In the opinions that he gives
He sees the world more critically
And sees life the way he lives

At times he needs to learn to take
A piece of humble pie
The best ideas are shared with others
Not just in his mind's eye

The musician who is quite advanced
Is one who'll analyze
And within the setting of the band
Open to compromise

It's hard for him at times to write
Music that he thinks
That at first glance, it may not be
Epiphany on the brink

Without learning all the aspects
Of respect, humility
He has mastered just the very start
Of musicality

Granted there is the technical side
To learning how to play
And the style in which he'll use a verse
Is varied day by day

But the worst mistake that he can make
In developing his ear
Is when music clouds the vision
Of opinions he's yet to hear

The Myriad of Objections

"To each his own" is a cliché well known
An opinion, I was taught, is to be left alone
For what is true for me may be for you, not
But I wonder how many is the myriad of objections
That have been crafted to stave off the Truth that seeks our affections

The Mind, intellectual, says that truth is your own
So you'd better not press it on mine
And intolerance is such an offense to cast blame
On Diversity's throne in our time

The Will, to be certain, in seeking pleasure or love
Or fulfillment in work or effort
Says that it's my life, my rights, my choice what I do
As long as I'm happy why should it hurt you

The Heart, ever pining, to find at the end of the rainbow
The great Reward shining
With whomever, however, and in any way that it can
Don't you know, haven't you heard
That above all deceit
Is the heart of mankind left to pine all alone

Oh, the myriad is much wider and deeper
Every reason explained, each excuse with its roots
But what they don't know is that all they've been searching
Striving and spending their life to gain
Is answered in the Truth to which all along, been objecting
That wonderful, loving Redeemer the same
One and only, Christ Jesus the King

Shadows and Mist

If you took all the tenderness of a mother's care
And with it the peace of a moonlit night's still air
If you gathered up the joy of a newborn child
Or counted the smiles from a toddler's face
If you saved every glimpse of better days
And each time something lasting touched your heart
It would only be a shadow of a reflection
Of what spans the heart of God

You could pool together love from ten thousand newlyweds
And add to it the bonds of lifelong friends
If you could muster all encouragement that a trusted mentor gives
It would still only be a mist
of the rain of Heaven's grace

For who He is, and what He is, is Love—perfect and pure
Every thought and deed of all that is good
Every simple joy from all that life is
It's all just a glimpse of our Creator's face
A mirror to the soul of He that put the stars in place
He that gave us breath, and joys of life
Meant for us to be in His family
To fill the empty space

The Master's Hands

There is a joy I want you to know
And a place I wish you to go
If you'll follow me toward the Father's arms
All the riches of His love He'll show

I hope and long that you would be
In paradise at Jesus' feet
His promises are always kept
I pray, join me in Eternity

More enticing than a stolen glance
More attractive than Hollywood romance
Would love for Him in your heart be
To me, please will you take a chance

At letting Him control your life
And setting all the wrongs to right
Cutting away all worthless strife
A new heart and life He'll give

Oh, now won't you please understand
That for our lives He has a plan
That He loves you more than I ever can
Put your life in the Master's hands

The Heart of God

My joy gave way to fear, as I pondered day's events
The uncertainty of the future held me in grave suspense
But the moment I did pray, and let my thoughts be heard
The anxiety within vanished at my first word
'Twas then I knew the thief had come to steal away my joy
He'd come to take away my peace, and promised pain along the way
But once again my God became my refuge and my strength
The thought of getting hurt gave way to simple words of praise
I can't thank the Lord enough, for peace within my heart
I know my tendency to worry, and to over-think each thought
But what weakness that may be in the fiber of my soul
Was meant to show the heart of God
Who longs to make me whole

The God Who Weeps

The mountains and the sea You formed with ease
From dust we came, with air to breathe
The stars, innumerable, in the sky
Impress me less than tears I've made You cry

My Father in heaven, how great in many ways
You set the earth to spin, lit the sun ablaze
If I felt the depth of pain that Your heart feels each day
I'd be amazed

Inside of us a soul is formed within
From the miracle of birth, to our slavery in sin
No such creature in the universe
Have You made but what wonder I do have
Not at the sunset's glow, nor at the thunder's mighty blow
But for how You weep each day
For the woman, once confessing
Now has since left her love for You
For the man, pushing You aside
To write his own life's truth
For the daughter, once enamored
With the thoughts of a loving God
Now has let life's worries crowd You
From whence You had stood in her, tall
To the son, still holding on
To truths as ever constant
Still he holds on to favorite sins
Love for You grows faintly
If any, or not at all

These are the hearts You long to capture
The waywardness You seek to tame
For life and death are within Your hands
It is this reason that You came

To seek and save that which was lost
To give life unto the full
You have the very Name that saves
That toward Your heart does pull

Tears

If I haven't tears in my eyes
Let them hear tears in my voice
Let their hearts be filled with anguish
Over the sins they've made by choice

Let them know You're the way out
From where they will end up
Let them wail and weep, cry and shout
Until communion with Your cup

I haven't got what it takes to change
It's a gift You gave
When I was wasting away
Your hand came down to save

I haven't got what it takes to serve
Deliver them from what they deserve
They've got to know they've made You cry
Until their own tears fill their eyes

Your hand comes down with anger
And leaves them barely alive
Let them know that to pain, you're no stranger
And through the tears they'll see the light

IV

Calling Out

Be hopeful in morning, for your prayers have gone out, and the day is not done.

Be hopeful in evening, for your prayers have gone out, and a new day will come.

Morning Prayer

Remind me, Lord, for by morning I have forgotten Your ways. Remind me, Lord, by daybreak my purpose has left me. Remind me, Father, to pray earnestly for others, to live in humble, joyful obedience and purity, to seek Your wisdom in Your word, and seek Your kingdom and Your righteousness above all things.

And Father, give me today the strength and desire to walk by Your Spirit, and the discipline to do so when I have no strength or desire at all.

Remind me, Father, so I do not forget my course, my reason, my resolve.

Speak to Me

Lord, speak to me. I've been called to Your service, to do the tasks You've set before me.

Lord, You're asking me, *"Why? Why do you insist upon living most of your life unchanged and peaking in "goodness" only on Sunday mornings? They're watching you. More than you realize. They may even look up to you. But your example is spotted with inconsistencies. If you will let me have first place in your life, I will make those inconsistencies come to the surface of your knowledge, and give you the strength to root them out for good.*
"Remember, you are my warrior placed to battle in the field of friends and family of which I've surrounded you. The enemy would like nothing more than to keep things just as they are. Don't give place to stagnancy, or fear of change, or fear of arguments or rejection when you feel my Spirit prodding you. They need to know the crux of my message, the reality of my existence, the truth of my love, even to the point of death on their behalf, and their desperate need for me. Because without the acceptance of the shed blood of my Son, they will not see life, but only death, pain, sorrow, and eternal lament. You are the one I've chosen to give light into their lives. This is the charge I have given you. Be obedient and faithful and patient; watch me work miracles out of what seems so far away! I desire to bless all of you, but you must first seek me. Know that I love you, and I'm with you always. I love you, my son."

Broken Shell

Look upon this broken shell, this weak man, with mercy and favor. Let me find strength again, from the unending source of Your refreshing waters. Let me find the strength to have victory after victory, battle after battle. May Your spirit be shed upon me once more; may You give me nourishment to my soul.

Father, reorganize and prioritize my life. Jesus, I am yours.

Remove my transgressions. Wash them away with a flood of Your grace, by the power of Your shed blood on the cross, shed to save, shed to show me, Your love can save me, by grace in blood, bathed me.

Jesus, restore my soul. I am without any energy to live for You. So I call upon Your name, ask to be imparted with Your breath of life, anew.

Undeserved Love

Father, what do You see when You look at me?

I see a man with a tender heart, a man who treasures his family, his friends, a man who longs to love his wife someday, but does not know her yet. I see a man after my own heart, full of compassion and goodness, strength, and mercy, one who will not quit, one who will not give in. I see strength in you; you will make it. You have what it takes. I see a man who is learning to love me, and who does love me, and in whom I am well pleased. I see my son. And I love him very much. I am grateful to have such a son.

Don't feel uncertain of my words. The enemy wants you to remain unsure of yourself, questioning your worthiness, wondering if you've been forgiven, and given strength. He wants you to be uncertain, wandering, straying, questioning, and guilty. He wants you to stay guilty. But you are not. I have set you free-past tense! It has been done! It is finished. You need only to remain in me and to follow after me, and you will remain free indeed. Rest in me when you are weary, eat and drink, when you're in need. I am the source of all life, the God of Jacob, the God of Abraham, Lord of all heaven and earth, creator of all things seen and unseen. Place your faith in me, dear son. I will never disappoint you, never leave you for another, never betray you.

I do trust you, Jesus. Thank you for such undeserved love.

Your words are like rain on my parched soul, and it forms in me a pool of rushing water that heals me, and flows from my eyes.

The Glory of a Heart Alive

Father in heaven, restore my soul and the glory of a heart alive. Give to me a clarity of the war in which we dwell. Create in me a strength to overcome my foes. I need to be reminded of my place within Your plan. It is a battle-plan to overthrow the enemy.

Lord, I have allowed him to steal so much—so much that I don't fully realize how much I've really lost. So much of life awaits me, and so much waits to be regained and restored. Make my path of life clear to me. Spread out before me a vision of Your glory manifest in my life. Restore to me a song in my heart.

You have heard my prayers. You have seen my tears, and lamented with me in my shame. I have known much shame—all of this You did not intend, but to use it for my good. Sever every tie and shut every door that has been allowed as enemy supply lines to keep me in sin. Create new inroads of Your goodness and mercy and the power of Your truth to replace what territory I have given to the enemy. Demolish every stronghold that wars against me, and set up Your fortress within, without, and surrounding me, Father.

There is so much I want for my life, and so much You desire to give me. Do not hold back Your goodness and blessings from me. Give me victory over my iniquity, and triumph over my willful disobedience, that I may please You, and that You may look upon me with favor.

For One Such as I

"You have so many questions, my son, and all will be answered in time. Yes, I have been preparing you, even as others around you have had their relationships for many months, so I have saved the months and years to come with the one I've set aside for you to be more blessed than you can imagine. Do not lose heart, my son. Continue in striving to be all I've called you to be. She is near now; you will know her soon. Don't worry, but instead take all concerns to me, for I will listen to each one and consider it carefully. Know that I love you, and that you have not been overlooked. I have heard your cries, and have seen your tears."

Oh, Father, how I trust in your love. You have only the best plans for my life, and if I am to miss out on something You intended to give me, it is my fault, not Yours, Lord. Jesus, the Name above all names, Creator of the whole universe, and billions of human beings, You are still able to care for one such as I, who must tire Your ear with incessant prayers for my future wife. My longing to know her has reached certain culmination, I hope. I hope and pray that I may not shed one more tear of sorrow or loneliness, enduring my singleness. Father, reveal Your plans in this to me. I offer You all my longings and put my fragile heart in Your care. May I find in You a constancy that no earthly love can fulfill.

Thank you so very much, Jesus, for all You are, and all You've done, and all You've given, and all You've yet to do and to give. May my life be a testimony of all you wish to give—which is a love unsurpassed—to each precious human.

A Simple Prayer

Father,

I come to You, a sinner, saved by grace, in need of You. I need to learn to love You with all of my heart. I need You to tear down strongholds of sin in my life, and replace them with wellsprings of living water. I need to come more often, like now, into Your presence. I need You to be my first love. I need You to create within me a thirst and a hunger for Your word. Lord, work these things in my heart, I pray, that I may live in gratitude and praise for what You've done, for who You are, and for what You have yet to do.

Thank You so much, Jesus. You are indeed precious to me, and Your Spirit so tender and patient. You fill me with peace, and give me hope. Your love radiates around me, and fills the longing of my soul. I am in need of nothing else when I'm in Your holy presence.

. . . whoever drinks the water I will give him will never thirst.
John 4:14

Solace

Thank You for the peace You bring
Before the storm has calmed

Thank You for the hope You give
When everything is still wrong

And as You go before me, Lord
As You prepare the way

I trust Your plan is larger than
The worries of today

V

Inside and Outward

Real love must be bound by truth, and truth, if it is palatable, must be bound by love.

Missing What Matters

The heart of a man is wayward and fickle
It shifts and changes like the sunset,
Right before your eyes, before you could even notice it

Man is fortunate to have a God and friend in one,
Who cares about his life, right down to the details,
And who does not let him trust his own judgment

Oh what folly it would be to live a lifetime,
Trusting one's own judgment, and living
Solely out of one's own conclusions

How much we would truly miss

What team do you play for?

The question begs to unveil the larger picture. This is no individual effort. There is no lone ranger. The greater good is more important than individual gain. My Father's cheering me on. He is so proud of His son, not because of his own success, but because His Father knows his heart will never give up, even after he has failed.

There is nothing like a father's love. It is that approval for which we long, inside our hearts. The healing power of the Heavenly Father can do more than we can imagine.

The Good Stored Up

" . . . for out of the overflow of the heart, the
mouth speaks . . . ."—Matthew 12:33-37

This verse strikes me as profoundly simple. Everyone knows that if you practice something, you'll get better at it, whatever it may be. Training, as we sometimes call it. So isn't it just the same to expect a person who engages in every kind of immorality to become so fluent in sin that it is always on their mouth, and their actions will reflect what they have stored up in their heart? Indeed, it seems to me just the same. Make no mistake that every sin drives us farther from a relationship with God, but it is comforting to know that we are never out of His grasp of love, mercy, grace, and strength. And so we find the need to live lives more pleasing to Him, in order that our relationship with Him might be stronger and mutually beneficial to us and those around us, and to repent when that relationship has faltered. We must remember that no man is an island. There are lives at stake all around us. Our relationship with God must be intact if we are to be effective at leading the lost to Him, and not ineffective in keeping our spiritual fervor. The most liberating thing the lifelong Christian finds after he has begun to mature in his faith, is that his real self begins to shine through. The double-mindedness subsides, the false "niceties" become genuine friendships, the tongue no longer needs to hide its other self among fairer company. What we become in character, out of the good stored up because of the change Jesus brings within us, is who we were always meant to be. And how else will this world see the truth, if not displayed from genuine hearts in genuine people?

Our Inherited Nobility

The great calling of God in each person's life begins with the realization that if we have come to the Lord by faith, our heart, once deceitful and wicked above all things, scripture tells us, is now inherently good. Our sinful nature is no longer our true nature anymore. Our true nature is defined by living out the potential of all that we are within. If a man lives by his flesh, by his carnal desires, he shall fulfill a potential for what is gained by evil deeds—hurt, pain, emptiness, addiction, possibly even prison, and eventually if he does not repent before the Lord, eternal death. But if a man, who has been made a dwelling place of the Spirit of God through his coming to faith in Christ, should live out his true nature, the potential is limitless, unending, and can only bring fulfillment, wholeness, joy, wisdom (and all of the fruits of the Spirit), and eternal life, which does not begin when we physically die, but which has already begun in receiving Christ's freedom from death which He hath bought with His life on the cross. We must, at all costs, seek to remember each day who we really are—an heir of God, a child of the King, possessing a good and noble heart, because we have taken on His character. And we must seek to live by this true nature, to understand that our hearts are good because He has transformed it. No Christian need ever think himself a sinner (though Christians certainly do sin)—he is of a noble line of God's allies, the Saints. He must simply begin to live like it.

The Drive to Change

What is it that drives a person to change who and what they are? Is it frustration? Is it maturity? Why is it, that we have constant struggle within ourselves that won't die until it has served its purpose: to make change? I have felt heartache. I have felt depression. I have felt severe frustration and lack of control. I've stumbled through hazy days of slow or no progress, and many days when everything is wrong and out of place. These things are my purpose, my reason, for change. For what it is that we wish to make happen is birthed only with meaningful purpose.

So many times have I been exhausted . . . and in need of taking time away. So many times I thought to start over again, with a new hope, yet made it a shorter distance along than before. The idea is conceivable, that if one wishes to make change, from the fire in their spirit, they shall, if so determined.

Let us look to God, so that all things may fall into place. And do not lose hope, for troublesome times grant maturity, knowledge, and personal growth.

A Beautiful Life

Life . . . in all its complexities, often makes me weary, and though I will always find solace and meaning because of its Creator, because of whom I've been endowed with certain currently unattainable longings, dreams, and desires—the type of which make me lonely, or hopeful, depending on the day or hour. If I may speculate, and hope and dream just once more, Lord, allow me to sum up these human and honest trappings . . . .

Devotion . . . utterly without end, unequivocal, unparalleled, and fervently grounded in the most perfect of all potentials: God's will. A love more constant than should be allowed in such a silly, fallen, human race, as it threatens to grasp within arms length of our Savior's dying love, although I know this to be certain exaggeration. Belief in the incredible, the astonishing, and the very possible result of man's potential, resolving never to abandon that to which has been loved and committed.

How perfect a life to hope for. How far from reality to dream. But I ask the Father in Jesus' name for one thing above all for my future: a wife beyond compare, and to be made a husband deserving of her.

He who finds a wife finds what is good and receives favor from the Lord.
Proverbs 18:22

Life Abundant

I think a big part of having real joy and peace within, comes from believing that God is on your side, that all of your hopes and longings and dreams—all that you desire in life, to bring you fulfillment—God is just waiting to provide. The problem is that our sin gets in the way—our pride, our selfishness, our stubborn ways. We will always be loved by God, but if we remain in sin after it has been shown to us, we will not have God's favor. God's storehouse of blessings will remain locked. Remember, Jesus didn't come to earth to "save us from our sins". To be sure, Jesus did die and rise to life to break sin's power and the power of death, but that is only part of a greater reason as to why God sent His Son to earth . . . "I have come that you may have life, and life abundant." Life—and life abundant; life to the very fullest it can be experienced. Isn't that what each of us really wants, when it comes right down to it?

The biggest lie of Satan is that he makes us believe God is simply angry with us sinners, and all too willing to throw us into hell for our disobedience, and that any chance at a happy and full life must be lived as far as possible from the constricting mores and rules of "God-dictatorship". What a sad and terrible lie to believe. The truth is, God wants nothing more than to see His beloved children love Him back, and to spend eternity with us in paradise. Our Father delights in our joy. He wants us to have good things, but He wants us to love and obey Him first, trusting in Him to take care of every need, every hope, every prayer. When we believe that what is best for our lives is going God's way, we will never again feel deprived at what sinful pleasures we may give up, because our faith remains intact. We can believe with hope in our hearts as David did, in Psalm 37, verse 4, "Delight yourself in the Lord, and He will give you the desires of your heart." Yes, to those who delight in doing God's work, in being obedient to Him, in reaching out to those with needs around us, God will grant the desires of their hearts.

So Much More

I find my soul is at peace in the times when it is touched by this world. I see so much that breaks my heart, in lives that are wasted, fallacies learned and regurgitated. Lies, lies, lies. Hardened hearts, people without direction. Precious lives tarnished and lost. Hurting people, hardened hearts, prideful, without compassion, quick to blame, quick to hate. No understanding, and no time for listening, because this world is all too fast-paced, and the almighty dollar rules the budgeting of our time and resources.

How few are those who seek to break the pattern, beginning with their own self inventory, a mirror to the soul by the Law and life of Jesus Christ. Self-help and support groups can only do so much. Most lack the capacity to incite positive change on their own. Even so, sin is not forgiven and wiped away in 12 steps, nor by the enlightenment of meditation, neither by the illusion of being a "good person". We cannot save ourselves, and we cannot save others. We are not able to fulfill our debt to God in our selfish ways, except with our very lives. In short, the blunt truth is that we deserve hell.

There is only one way to escape our fate. Jesus Christ, the source of all that is truly good, has already paid our debt by His own sacrifice, even under excruciating physical and emotional pain on the cross. And He did it for everyone, from the person who doesn't see themselves as all that bad at all, to the very worst of humanity. For every awful thing we do, even continually, even while we are under the knowledge of our wrongdoing, Jesus seeks to rescue us. This, my friends, is love. A love that has no equal in all the universe, that is, the Creator's love for His chosen and most precious creation: us. I think we do not often enough think of ourselves as creation. But in the Maker's eyes we are more precious than life-giving air to breathe, more beautiful than a desert sunset, more grand than the tallest mountain; He sees in each and every one of us incredible potential, to be all that we have been created to be, and to receive all we have been chosen to receive. His blessings are endless.

But we cannot receive from Him unless we first receive Jesus. His son, God's own son, is the difference between spending our eternity in heaven or in hell. Jesus is the difference; His death and resurrection is what separates Christianity from Islam, Buddhism, Hinduism, and the countless other world religions. Yes, Christianity is much more than religion. It is much more than a way of life, or set of rules. It is our reconciliation to our Creator, whom we have wronged through our sinful, selfish nature.

God waits with loving arms to tell you that He loves you without condition, and more than you will ever know. God may be tugging at your heart right at this moment. Your soul, your life depends on how you respond to that tugging, whether you decide to bury it, or dig down and uncover it. Those who have the seeker's heart will find God, the Bible tells us. Don't resist Him. He has your best interests at heart, and storehouses of wonderful things He wants to give you if you'll follow Him. The most wonderful of all is eternal life—an escape from the death penalty our evil ways have earned us. Think of it . . . life unending, without pain or tears, shame or fear. Heaven—in every sense of the word, greater than we can imagine it to be. A gift we can all receive, but which none deserve. Don't put off coming to terms with your truthful state before God. We are all in need of Him. Will you let His Law condemn you on the Day of Judgment, or will His grace sustain you and bring you into eternal life? Let the 10 Commandments show you that you have sinned . . . .

Have you ever lied, even once? Then by your own admission you are guilty before a Holy God, and can have no place in His kingdom. Have you ever stolen, regardless of value? Then you are a thief, and deserve eternal punishment in the lake of fire.

You may think the punishment is far greater than the crime. But it isn't to a Holy God who cannot tolerate sin. Just as a good judge sentences a serial killer or rapist to many, many years in prison, so an offense against God, even once, is a serious one, and must be punished by death. That is how His Holiness contrasts to our sinfulness. That is how serious sin is, and why it took His only Son to die to save us.

Something may be restless within you, is it not? Something about hearing of your own guilt makes you uncomfortable, almost angry. But that is the purpose of guilt—to make us aware we've done wrong. And guilt is made known by the Law, to show us our true state before God. We have only yet looked at two of the ten commands, and surely you must admit in all honesty that you're at fault in at least one of those areas. This means you are in need of God's grace, which is His power to forgive. You need Him to clear the slate, and remove your awaiting punishment. Ask Him now to cleanse you, and to change your life for the better. Ask Jesus to live within your heart, so you might now begin to give back to this loving God who has done so much for you already, even to the point of sending His son to suffer and die on a cross to pay your ransom from death's waiting grip. Eternal life is promised by God to all who make this decision, and begin the process of letting God remove your old sinful ways and habits. May God never give you another night's rest until you've surrendered your life to Him.

"For he who wishes to save his way of life will lose it, yet he who is willing to lose his life for my sake, will gain it."
Luke 9:24

For All Mankind

What is diligence? What is persistence, resolve, honor, and duty? Most of the time, it is without glory or fanfare, without cheers or encouragement. It is the stuff of life: the mundane, the stressful, the routine . . . there is much pain in waiting, much patience needed in our hope, much shame when we sin, for we understand that the stakes could not be higher. We are outnumbered, both in populous and popular opinion. But our Commander has called us to act above the changing tides of changing times, and to live out His directives with diligent obedience. All around us, the souls of thousands are in danger. We must be a beacon of truth, hope, and goodness in this fallen world. How can we save ourselves, and not our neighbor? Is he or she not loved with the same fervor by our Lord, our mutual Maker? Did not Christ's stripes bleed for ours and their salvation also? Did not Jesus spill His blood for the sins of not only the few, or the good, or the evil, the repentant or the unrepentant, but for all mankind? His gift is not earned, nor can it be. We must act as ambassadors of freedom to those in slavery to sin, whose very eternity is doomed without the cross of Christ. May we who are called to lead this generation of souls into the Kingdom of God, be ever praying for courage and strength to live out our calling in the army of God with diligence, persistence, resolve, and honor, to the fulfillment of our duty here on earth.

Insight From the Author

Life is easier to live when you live it the way God gives it . . .
. . . one minute, one hour, one day at a time.

Righteousness is a double-edged sword
Seeking after it is the first blade
The second is its reward

God is the author of life, so it's no surprise that when . . .
We're in battle, He's in our corner
We need guidance, He's our mentor
We need motivation, He's our coach
We are suffering, He's our friend
We have failed, He's our confidant
We cry, He cries too.

Virtues Revered

Honor. Beauty. Few things are as revered as these. They are enduring, almost timeless. And yet our Lord encompasses both, and has infinite resources to bestow them. Such beauty and honor that we may ever behold, can only come from the abundant radiance of pure goodness that is our Father, God, and His Son, who is Christ the Lord. Praise be to You, Father, and glory and honor due Your name.

> Tossed about by waves
> Of "feel-like" I am driven
> Jesus makes me whole

A Beautiful World

When one looks long enough, and settles one's breath just long enough to see a moment of beauty amidst the counterfeit and crude reflection of what we were meant to be, a comparison can be made of what tainted beauty this world yet holds, though selfish lust is the currency we spend at our own debt, to the undistorted vision of God in His perfect goodness.

If we could comprehend the breadth of our fallen state as a race once bearing the image of our Creator, could we then contain in the capacity within human reason the enormous possibilities of what man could have been, had we never fallen?

How skewed has our morality become, when Christ's name is blasphemed so carelessly, that the world sees it less offensive to use God's name in vain rather than a common curse word.

. . . though I have fallen, I will rise. Though I sit
in darkness, the Lord will be my light.
Micah 7:8

Praying for God's Best

What may be God's best for you, is not always what *you* might think is best. What *is* His best, is what glorifies Him the most. And how does He show His glory? Redemption. Making new what is old. Bringing hope to the hopeless. Redeeming, restoring, and transforming lives. So what seems so far away, so hopeless? It may be God's best to use it, and turn it all around.

Not Just Mysterious

To ascribe to God credit for things He's done in our lives, with only the implication of the miraculous or supernatural, and without inclusion of the practical or even routine, is to place God in all too small a box, and does not allow the full nature of God to be expressed. Since when does it not become God's handwriting if it can be explained or reasoned? Must God, being supernatural, only work His purposes through that which is supernatural? Cannot He be allowed to work in practical and explicable situations? Certainly God can work in any way He so chooses. It is erroneous to think God must *only* work in mysterious ways.

The Heart of God's Law

Perhaps one of the biggest misconceptions about God from non-Christians is over the idea of His law being some heavy-handed rule book of do's and don'ts, with the threat of punishment—ultimately, hell—at the end. What most of secularized society fails to understand is the incredible love and goodness behind each command. The unbeliever has believed a great many set of lies that are tied to the one belief that his life is best left to be run by himself alone, on his terms. His belief system may go something like this: "It's smart to live with someone before getting married to them, because you can 'try before you buy'; it's just common sense". In reality, God's command against such behavior—which many call prudish or old fashioned, is actually how romantic relationships are best fulfilled and experienced. Many see the Bible's stance on homosexuality as intolerant and even hateful. But again, they misunderstand that since God is a God of love, all His commands are rooted in love, and are in our best interest, and He is therefore warning us that the gay lifestyle is much less than fulfilling. Most of society fails to see the connection between Jesus' words, "I have come that you may have life, and have it to the full", and what He says about how we are to live.

We all desire fulfillment in life—in our goals, our hopes and dreams, and in our relationships. It is indeed sad that many see God's commands as restrictive to their freedom to pursue fulfillment, when in reality His rules serve as a guide to provide us every good thing we were meant to experience. The truth is, God is NOT out to spoil our fun. God is on the side of pleasure. Intrinsic to each and every law, every command, every word offered as wisdom in the Bible is out of His great desire to see us live as all we were meant to live. Remember, it was sin—going against God's commands by living our own way—that got us kicked out of the Garden of Eden, a place created to be our paradise.

It doesn't get too much clearer than that in scripture: paradise is where God intends for us to be, and we will have it when we live in harmony with Him. But too often our sin gets in the way, and we miss out on countless blessings that He is just waiting to give to us. I hope I will never know just what I have missed out on because of my sin. Fulfillment, life-abundant—it's just waiting for us, friend. But we've got a deadly disease called sin, and it can't be cured except by getting a new heart, and that can only come from Jesus.

Take up Your Cross

To take up your cross each day—what quality does that signify? Humility. And why does the cross bring humility? Because it is a heavy burden that we cannot bear, which is the burden of our slavery to sin (Galatians 5:1). And how are we to remind ourselves daily of just how great a burden our sin is? By our communion with our Lord in prayer, in steadfast obedience, in reading His truth in His Word, the Bible. To do these things, is to take up our cross daily.

A Life Well Lived

The Christian of today does not defend his faith because he doesn't know if he really believes it, and he cannot defend his faith because his life lacks the example of it. If we are to give solid testimony of God, and His truth, our lives must stand up to scrutiny. As someone once said, one cannot argue with a life well lived.

The Dream Aspired

I wonder sometimes if I'm going through a new period of introspection and ultimately improvement. While many things that are still anchors to my success in life remain, I find my disdain for them growing, and a yearning within to see the potential revealed for my life as the Lord intends it. There is much to lament and feel self-pity over, if I am to dwell on such things, and I often do. I am still alone, without a significant other, as most of my life has been. I have never had a romantic relationship last more than a month, and the sum of all my relationships amounts to much less than 5 months. I am still in debt, thousands of dollars. I can't scrape enough money to buy a decent vehicle, so I borrow it. But I can't even borrow it on my own, without Dad's help. I am working 2 jobs to make ends meet, and though I am thankful for them, I feel they are far less than reaching my value in this world. I feel almost wasted in them, but on the other hand, somehow humbled, because I know I have not given myself fully to the Lord, and I am certain He has kept opportunities from me as a result.

I don't want a wasted life. I always thought, in my youth, that I would amount to very much in the world. I had so many aspirations, as I still do, but they are somewhat unfocused, and so far, unfulfilled. It's as though I'm having a pre-mid-life crisis, realizing I'm a chronic underachiever.

Deep down I feel God has made me unique. I feel I have been blessed with a great many talents, and I am ashamed to have wasted much of them up to this point in time. Perhaps it is simply delusions of grandeur, but I feel inside that I was made for more, and that is why I have such dreams within me.

At the root of it all, I know my shortcomings are nothing less and nothing more than sin. I have allowed Satan free reign over much of my life, and I continue to let him steal away my inheritance as a child of God. The understanding that my failures have caused my discontented place in life is only more coal heaped upon my head, and it weighs on me. It weighs on my conscience, and my spirit, and it nearly squelches my passions. I hope for so much in this world, and to be a blessing to God and to others. I want a life of grandeur. I don't know how to get it . . . I think I often just felt it would land at my feet—God made me gifted so why not? He can make the chances to use the gifts appear. But I know that what character is yet being cultivated is like the winter before the frost breaks and opens the ground to be tilled and sown once more. I've got work to do, and it begins in my heart, in dealing with my sin, and my relationship with Jesus. Often it is difficult to even see beyond my circumstances—not because I can't, but because I don't want to. I'm not certain why, but it's true. It's as if I'm afraid of finding the answer, because it means I can't live lazily any more. It means I have to ante up and kick in, like a man, and take responsibility for the calling of God upon my life. Even my dreams are a burden to me—a burden to be fulfilled, and a mark of failure if they are not. But even as I realize this, I know it is one more thing I need not be burdened with; I have put it upon myself needlessly, when God's broad shoulders are meant to handle the load. It is what I give to Him: my submission . . . because I am nothing without Him. He who hath made me, desires to see His glory revealed through my life.

Catalyst of Change

I feel as though real change is going to begin in my life. I'm not sure just how, or which things, or when, but I know it must start with seeking God first, and striving for righteous living. When I finished making a list of prayer requests, I found a peace that felt like all my cares were upon God instead of me. I felt a glimpse of the fulfillment of those prayers, imagining them all coming to pass, and how I have virtually no other concerns aside from those desires of my heart that I have written. They sum up everything that means something to me. Though they are not all equal at all to each other, they are the most pressing, most important of my prayer requests to the Lord, and represent what I desire most in life.

> *"Put out into deep water, and let down the nets for a catch . . . ." When they had done so, they caught such a large number of fish that their nets began to break.*
> Luke 5:4, 6

From Truth to Conviction

In what way does change come about in a person's life? When God molds us, He does so usually very slowly, because He wants us to learn along the way. Most often, He does not simply take away our struggle, but prods us to work through it. It is first an undertaking of the mind—understanding truth in proper doctrine, as it applies to our struggles with sin. Repeated visitations to these truths birth knowledge of heart, where we can truly understand the implications of both adhering to and ignoring our new-found wisdom. But what really makes a lasting change within us, is when we have stuck to the truth long enough to see the mind-knowledge and heart-knowledge blended together, making the abstract combine with the tangible and practical, from which we derive a conviction. And a conviction within is a capstone to the foundations of the decisions we will make and the governing dynamics of how we will ultimately live.

A man is never more easily persuaded to do good, than
after you have first appealed to his conscience.

The Willing Heart

Years has it taken for me to come to this: a place where I am now becoming useful. So many countless days wasted and empty. Futile were my longings, when I did not bring them to You. Why has it taken this long, Lord, for me to truly seek You? I am only now becoming soft for You to mold me.

As a child of five, I asked Jesus into my heart. With Christian parents, I went to church every week. But for all those years, my faith was almost completely limited to the hour or so on Sunday morning. And I was left with a vague sense of your truth and reality, with little bearing on how I lived my life.

As a young teenager, through the character-building insecurities and ridicule of my youth, You began to bring out the unique person within me. Through short-lived yet deeply impacting relationships, You plowed the tough ground of my heart, and begged me to let go of the tight grasp of my life's control. Through recent years, and with prayers from my mother, I'm sure, and through the truths You've helped me to see, and a heart that has begun to desire more of You, I questioned my salvation. Not in such a way to discredit Jesus' sacrifice for my sin, but to affirm my own priorities in life, and to examine myself in the way that "a good tree will bear good fruit", and testing to see if I was "in the faith".

Lord, You have helped me to realize that a person with head-knowledge of You, yet no heart-knowledge is not a true Christian at all. The good tree of the truly born again convert is in his ongoing and developing relationship with Jesus, his heart for greater knowledge and discernment, a giving of his life's control over to the Holy Spirit to guide him, as evidenced by changes in behavior subject to the obedience to Christ, and the pursuit and maintenance of making God the number one priority. The heart truly converted will also be filled with compassion for those yet in darkness, who await God's just and eternal punishment. And there will be fellowship with other believers in the church, and a peace beyond understanding.

Therefore, I believe true conversion to contain the following:

1. Sincere confession of sins to God, asking for His control over one's life.
2. Belief in the Bible and all of God's promises, and in all He has done, especially the death and resurrection of Jesus for the forgiveness of sins.
3. Seeking to know God and to become more like Jesus, and to do His will, by reaching out to others with the Truth.

These points can then be broken down into what I call the Seven Tenets of Christian Living. The Holy Spirit revealed these truths to me one day, as I was heading home between church services.

> Communion—time spent one on one with God in prayer, confession, petition, intercession, praise, and thankfulness.
>
> Fellowship—encouraging and enjoying time with friends and other believers in the church, strengthening each other.
>
> Worship—a spirit of joy, giving God praise for all He's done; it's where we give back to God in honor of what He's given us.
>
> Instruction—feeding on God's truths.
>
> Obedience—public and private decisions of faith, doing what's right even when no one notices but God, even when we are weak.
>
> Evangelism—reaching others who are lost and condemned without Christ
>
> Discipline—setting apart the time and energy to do all of the above.

So, in all of these, can it be determined which is most important of the seven? Consider that without communion, our spiritual fire will go out. Without instruction, we gather no fuel for the fire. Without worship, we will lose our joy and hope. Without fellowship, we become isolated and easily ensnared by sin. Without obedience, our witness to others is hindered, and our growth in our relationship with God is stunted. Without evangelism, our focus is lost, and our work is in vain. And without discipline, we cannot accomplish any of the above. It should be said also, that without God's spirit moving in our hearts, we can do none of the above, because spiritual disciplines are spiritually accomplished.

So how do we recognize true conversion? "By their fruit you will recognize them. Do people pick grapes form among thorns, or figs from thistles? Likewise, every tree bears good fruit, and every bad tree will bear bad fruit." (Mathew 7:16-17)

Therefore, "Every tree that does not bear good fruit will be cut down and thrown into the fire." (Mathew 7:19)

Are we then saved by our own "good fruit"? No! Rather by our faith in the grace of God, through accepting the atonement for our sin in the sacrifice of His son Jesus on the cross. The fruit of our lives will be the evidence, merely, of a true or a false conversion. So, ask yourself this question: does the evidence of your life favor that you have been truly converted, as a follower of Jesus? Ask yourself this now, on this side of eternity, while there is still time. It's the most important self-evaluation there is, especially when your very soul is at stake.

The God Who Loves

God loves intensely His most precious creation—humankind. There is no wavering or shaking of this love; it is constant. There is nothing to earn this love; it is freely given because His very nature is love. There is nothing that can separate, break, cause to dwindle, or to put on hold this love; our greatest sins He will overlook if we will confess and repent of them. Nothing we can say or do can ever affect the constant flow of His love for us.

Consider if you will a man's deeply committed love for his wife; it would be hard to understand how a wife receiving such love would not reciprocate it. Yet, as sinful beings, we are just like that, until we come to know, in greater personal experience, the nature of love in our Heavenly Father.

Many might say, "Why does He love me? I don't want His love, I don't need it, I've never asked for it. I'm perfectly fine on my own. Thanks, but no, thanks." Imagine the heartache an estranged parent would feel if, after years of separation from their child, they are finally being reunited to them, yet those same words of indifference are spoken just as coldly by the child to the parent. Isn't this the very same thing God must endure from us, the creation made in His image? How can a parent not love his or her child, almost instinctively, from the moment the child is born? How then, also, would our Father in heaven, be able to withhold love from those He created specifically with which to have a close relationship?

How much needed guidance, wisdom, direction, good gifts, help, assistance, understanding, and love would a child miss out on by saying, "Thanks, but no, thanks. I don't need God in my life,"? Moreover, as sinful beings in need of a cure for the disease of sin that leads to death for all eternity, we need a Physician capable of healing us. God, the Great Physician, has such a cure for us, in the blood of Jesus, His son. How foolish to be afflicted with a life-threatening disease, and yet not accept the cure readily available to us.

Genuine Conversion

It's a hard question to ponder, to consider who is really saved, and who only thinks they are. I feel burdened, at times, to pray for a family member who is displaying a lack of the Spirit's fruit in their life, and I am quick to raise concern over their salvation. I do not think there is fault in this, however judgmental it may appear, because it is birthed in love and concern, and of intercession. But aside from having the mind of Christ, how can a person determine to have, at best, virtual certainty that another's soul is in danger? Let me offer an insight I feel God has given me:

Imagine the Christian life as a journey through prairie and stream, woods and thicket, sunshine and also rain. But throughout this journey, there remains a path, wherever it may go—even unto the darkness of a cavern or thick brush with vines and creepy, crawly things, the path remains clearly visible beneath one's feet. Since it could be taken as absurd to think God would condemn one of His "new creations" (that is, one whom God has forgiven and redeemed) for one solitary sin, it stands to reason that a pattern of unrepentant sins, or sins that increase rather than decrease, would be as if proving to God that one wished to live on his or her own terms, and not God's. In such a case, we can infer that a pattern of continual and unrepentant sinfulness shows the conversion was not genuine after all. We also know from scripture that God is slow to anger, so He must give us plenty of time and opportunity to show Him for whom we wish to live—ourselves, or for Him. So the conclusion I draw is this: a person, once believing in God, and moving forward on this path of life, who makes continual and habitual decisions to veer from the path, is likely in danger of proving that their salvation was never genuine, and their faith never real, because their works did not give evidence of the "fruit" of a converted person. If a person such as this never repents, then their work-less faith is of no use, and they were most likely a false convert, such as those Jesus spoke of in the parable of the sower. This parable talks of the stony ground, and ground with thorns, and the good soil—the first two being the heart of the false convert whose faith never developed roots or was choked out by this world.

I believe, then, that if God is just (and He is, according to His Word), He will give ample time for each soul to come to repentance before allowing them to die without forgiveness and therefore condemned forever to hell. Now, rightly so, only God can decide justly how much time and opportunity a person is given before it is deemed "too late", and their place in heaven, if they ever had one, is lost. This falls in line with what scripture speaks of as being "given over to sin", or when God "hardened their hearts". On God's time line, if we continually make decisions to exclude Him and His ways from our hearts, He will eventually-if our path in this regard remains unchanged-harden our hearts to Him, and we will be in grave danger of hell.

The choice to rebel always remains with us, as individuals, and we must continually seek to squelch the old nature of the flesh each day. That is why the apostle Paul exhorted us in 2 Corinthians 13:5, to "test ourselves to see if we are in the faith". We do not want to take our salvation for granted, thinking that "once a Christian, always a Christian", even if we make little or no effort to be obedient to that calling of righteous living. We mustn't be one of those Christ referred to as calling out, "Lord, Lord", but being one He never knew. Nor can we afford the risk of being called lukewarm, and being also spewed from His mouth. Let us continually seek to please God with holy living, not to justify ourselves by our good works, which is not possible anyhow, but to prove our salvation is indeed genuine, and our love for God, real.

VI

Roots Digging Deeper
Part Two

I will rest in You, Father
I will wait and be still
Whatever should happen
Let it be Your will

Transparent

Somehow my innocence is trampled
Underfoot of fleeted time
The laughter, though in good times
Is second best, I'd say

Where is it that I fit in, amidst this worldly fair
How can I be a beacon, I've shrugged for which I care
I agree that one must not take all so seriously
But I believe in that which is greater
There's more at stake than I can see

Let me offer this advice
Free of charge but not of study
We'd better know for sure if our lives are ours to live

I love family, friends, my passions too
But I lack all if I love not You
I can't but bow my head in shame
When I think of each time I've denied Your name
My Lord, my God please take away
My desire to make my own path this day

Bless Me, Jesus, Bless Me

Bless me, Jesus, bless me
Make me holy, filled, not empty
Sanctify the life You gave me
By Your blood that bought and bathed me

Bless me, Jesus, bless me
With favor do caress me
May I seek the One who sought me
And live in holy victory

Bless me, Jesus, bless me
Direct my path before Thee
Into Your hands I commit myself
To take leave of my iniquity

Bless me, Jesus, bless me
May I use the gifts given me
To serve, that others may see Thee
And store treasures for eternity

Bless me, Jesus, bless me
With my precious wife to be
Companion, lover, she will be
In You give us one unity

Bless me, Jesus, bless me
Make straight my way before me
That all the world may see Thee
The God of love and glory

May God be gracious to us and bless us and make his face shine upon us,
that your ways may be known on earth, your salvation among all nations.
Psalm 67:1

My True Love

The world holds gifts yet unknown to me
The greatest known is Christ, I believe
Yet how my life poorly reflects
My shaky love for Him, I must confess

Never will He hurt me, never will He leave
A love tested by death I can't fully conceive
I pray I'll be receptive to what the Lord will teach
I pray I'll love Him first and beyond
My short and weakened reach

Well of Grace

How deep Your well of grace, O Lord
Though we pile on offense
That builds up as a wall
Your grace it floods our stubborn ways
The well of grace is poured
Your nature that is love
The purest blood that flowed
To pay the debt I owe
'Tis mercy from above

Hope's Beacon

Is there not a hope within
When the times are lonely, and I feel the pull of sin
For what is unseen, the joy ahead
Gives hope in God's promises said
Yet at times like these I have often felt
Overwhelmed in a deep, dry well

Still, I find it is in my control
To take captive thoughts, to make them whole
When mostly as I dwell upon
My present state, hope's all but gone
So I mustn't focus on the here and now
Good things are coming, He will show me how
I am to be made worthy to receive these things
As You, my precious bride He'll bring

So I pray for God's sustaining power
To bring hope interminable
In this my darkest hour
He has not forgotten me, I know He hears my prayers
I am thankful for the peace He gives
And for just how much He cares

I am still confident of this: I will see the goodness of the Lord in the land of the living. Wait for the Lord; be strong and take heart, and wait for the Lord.
Proverbs 27:13-14

Almost Free

Almost free, out of the blue
Almost light, through a window's view
Seven times, seven crimes
Little less than no success
In a wading pool of past regrets
Tow the line and pass the test

If I'd take the road, take the leap
Bloodstained hands from what I reap
If I'd throw aside old habit's pride
I'd no longer need a place to hide

The horizon's face betrays a smile
If I'm not pure before You, go the extra mile
Then the stars will lose their shine
And I'll lose my place in line

If my world pivots not upon You
How can the yellow come from blue
Here I am at the threshold of decision
Don't let it slip from my life's vision

Therefore . . . let us throw off everything that hinders and the sin that so easily entangles, and let us run with perseverance the race marked out for us.
Hebrews 12:1

First in Line

When I find my heart troubled
A human trait in a human world
I now understand I rise and fall
With the tide of events unfurled

And so You've revealed in me
A heart in selfish idolatry
When I let desires and longings run me to and fro
My center torn by circumstantial blow
But now I see why You've designed
My heart to hold You first in line
That verse made clear as for the first time

If I would seek You above all else
They would for certain fall into place
You connect these things, and make them whole
For You have not given to me
A spirit of fear, dismay, worry
But of strength and power in Your Name
May I never be the same

Jesus, my rest I find in You
Take these burdens, long since due
Nail them with all sin to the cross to die
May I find my center in You, alive!
Your love makes all things perfect; on this I rely

How long have I held deep within
Romantic idolatry, never calling it sin
A marriage like so few have known
All prayers for blessings, love untold
This is only possible if I give my heart, the whole
To You, for out of constancy
A love more radiant that human love can be
Will flow these things I have long desired
And so, I lay down my precious hope
To find such love to whom I shall devote
And with Your guidance will I place
You, Father, in Your rightful place

First in line, from now on each day
Jesus, my rest, may I always say
You are the love I've searched for long
Teach me to seek You fervently strong
That these things, added unto me
Would take their place as less than Thee

Seek ye first the kingdom of God and his righteousness,
and all these things shall be added unto you.
Matthew 6:33

Oh Lord My Life

Oh Lord, my life, You came to earth to save me
To redeem me, to show me all life means to Thee
You desire I have life, and have it to the full
May You infuse me with the desire to see this through
That the prison I visit, and sometimes remain,
Would crumble to dust, and with it, my shame
May I find in You what life You promise,
And we that seek it with all effort within us

Take Your place in these gaps where sin had remained
And wash it anew by Your blood's holy stain
Fill in the emptiness that finds me wanting
When the means is the end, earthly pleasure becomes haunting
And by Your grace, as Your work refreshes
Fulfill the longing for earthly love that my bride now possesses
And I, who have spent so many nights praying
Would meet her soon and know it was worth all the waiting

Oh, Lord, my life, I pray You'd become
May I be fulfilled, and Your work for me, done
Before I leave this world behind
For paradise awaits, and true life, I will find

What's to Become

What's to become of me as I tread upon the road
Sifting through decision's sands, stopping to unload
Looking for an answer at each new turn I face
Wondering when the time will come
To take me from my place

Yearning to be different from the failures in my past
Asking for direction as my own will never last
Seeing one who captures the attention of my eye
Beauty upon beauty, to God, a distant cry
Longing to be learning, and hoping to be helped
Astray is where I'll find remorse
More worthless days I've felt

Strengthened by convictions and wisdom of the old
Obedience is gifted by the day when we are told
My life I've lain before you
Given up by my sheer love
Spread this word to all the world
Love comes from the Lord above

As He Did

I have lived a lie
Walking in the darkness my lips deny
He spoke in my defense
Still I choose independence
How can I proclaim His Name
If I live not the same
As He did

I aim, I strive to be
Built upon simple purity
Ageless and the same
Are words that leave no place to dismay
I want to live forever
So take away the love
For this world

I want to do as He did
I want to live as He lived
I want to share the grace He gives

I'll hold the torch to burn my hand
Sever the grip that breaks my stand
I'll stomp my foot on Satan's plan
Jesus, to do as You did

If anyone would come after me, he must deny himself
and take up his cross and follow me.
Mark 8:34

Don't Let Me

Don't let me whine and cry for food that doesn't last, nor satisfies
Don't let me wish upon a thought that hinders the wisdom You've taught
I can see clearly, I can see clearly, when You teach me
Don't let me turn back to the place of sin and shame
Don't let me join the ranks of leaders, until You say I'm ready
Show me how to be faithful in small things
So I might serve You in great ways
My spirit longs for blessing
First, remove this sin I'm confessing

I can see clearly, I can see You so clearly, when You humble me
I feel a smile within me 'cause I know that You aren't done with me
Make me everything I'm supposed to be

Don't let me lose my footing when those who know me are yet searching
Don't let me forget my calling to share Your truth in a world that's falling
Make me everything You've planned me to be
Make me everything I am to be
Let me serve You throughout eternity

But we have this treasure in jars of clay to show that this
all surpassing power is from God and not from us.
2 Corinthians 4:7

Called Me Back

Once so blind, I start to see
The many things You've done for me
I start to see I'm all alone
When I try to strike out on my own
You break the dam, and set me free
The tears show that I've hurt You deep

Then I heard the echoes strained
A voice inside, cast on me: blame
So I do hurry to Your side
Hear my cries as I confide
'Cause without You, I'm already dead
Wipe away with that You've bled

I heard a call, calling out to me
You're calling me back, and setting me free
No time to waste, there's work to do
Let me be Your mouth and hands
I'll do it all for You

Forgive me now, I do implore
Don't want to tread Your blood anymore
Don't want to throw down what I hold dear
Can't believe the wasted years
It seems that there is always one
Who leaves my heart as yet undone
So fill the space, and plug the void
Let her be my second joy

*Fight the good fight of the faith. Take hold of the
eternal life to which you were called . . . .*
1 Timothy 6:12

Less Than Me

When your eyes can only see
What's in front of you
It's a shame to me
I've missed out

If your mind cannot contain
A heaven without pain
I pity you
I'm afraid I've made the same mistake
Giving in to laziness
Accepting second rate

I'm sorry Lord, for the tears I've made You cry
For the days I've let this world surround me
I hadn't even thought about Thee
Accept from me
Apology
Don't let me die

I've eaten dust and dirt
When a feast was lain before me
I've brushed aside the helping hand
And drank iniquity
I've turned my head away from You
And reveled in the dark
I'm crying out to You, my God
Don't let me fall apart

Purpose Unfolding

The Lord has His purpose, even in these low times of life. He will build me up through it. One day, I will understand just what purpose all of this is serving. There are many details yet to unfold, and my story is not nearly finished—it is just beginning . . . .

He will restore my wasted years

He will replace my broken dreams

He will sustain me in painful hours

He will destroy the shameful towers

He will be my guiding flame

He will lead me home again

He will bring me to His best

He will heal me in His rest

He has ever heard my prayers

He will turn me from despair

He has boundless comfort still

Him, I trust, to do His will

He has seen the tears that fall

He will make sense of it all

He has ever been my guide

He will never leave my side

Days of Grace

You're cleaning up the clutter
And You've drawn me close to You
You're building up to something
For a future bright and new
I tremble with excitement
As Your will it shall unfold
As I learn to follow Your ways
Blessings begin to flow

Thank You for the peace You give
Thank You for the gift
Of shining Your light of truth
Into such a life as this

I thank You how You're using this
To mend the broken part
The places that we need to heal
You're drawing near our hearts
I'll keep praying as I have, my Lord
To see Your perfect will
The hopefulness within my heart
Has made the time stand still

I pray for days of grace ahead
And for the strength to stand
For a future yet unknown to me
I trust Your perfect plan

For I know the plans I have for you . . . plans to prosper you and
not to harm you, plans to give you hope and a future.
Jeremiah 29:11

In Due Time

Your grace will lead me home
For Your strength is made perfect in my weakness
Your hand of mercy is always upon me
It will never let me fall
I will lean upon Your grace so strong
I will give to You my all
No trial that comes will be my end
No struggle shall prevail
The Lord is a rock, my firm foundation
He is the strength of my soul
No thorn of flesh, no mind unsound
Shall unravel my faith
The Lord is a beacon of hope
A lighthouse of faith, a tower of love Divine
Unending is His house of grace
That will lift me in due time

My grace is sufficient for you, for my strength is made perfect in weakness.
2 Corinthians 12:9-10

Jesus, My Rest

Jesus, healer, savior, friend
Reach down to save me once again
I'm covered by the weight of sin
I've willingly left You, but as I turn, may I bless You
With a heart that can't find rest without You there

Jesus, comforter and king
This life has worn me down within
I have no strength left nor the will to carry on
I've often found myself in battle, laying down my arms

Jesus, redeemer of my soul
Give me Your grace and make me whole
I've been living so much less than what You have for me
Because You've set me free
Yet I continue now to linger, a captive no more,
But I daily revisit my chamber
What madness when a free man returns to shackles cold
For one drink of iniquity, a piece of me is sold

Jesus, lover of my heart
Creator of all that I art
Stay with me awhile, and sit beside me still
Wash away the troubles, and restore my broken will
Make me the man that You know I will become
When I surrender all of me to You

Come to me, all you who are weary and burdened, and I will give you rest.
Matthew 11:28

Transcendence

One more climb on mountaintop, to see the sun shine bright
It seems it's just a waste of time; I know what it looks like
But another truth has entered in to put me back in place
A conviction growing stronger now—have I got what it takes?

To think that all this time my prison walls were all a lie
The only thing that held me in was lack of faith to try
Because the debt's been paid, there no more need to serve another day
My freedom, life in victory, was bought by Jesus' grace

So how can I, in freedom, live as one still hung to chains?
And what ingratitude could trample blood shed for my wicked ways?
Only fools despise a feast delayed by trading for mere crumbs
I pray I'll be a fool no more, this time past setting sun